HOUSE PLANTED

CHOOSING, GROWING,
AND STYLING THE
PERFECT PLANTS
FOR YOUR SPACE

HOUSE
PLANTED

LISA MUÑOZ

PHOTOGRAPHY BY
ERIN KUNKEL

TEN SPEED PRESS
California | New York

CONTENTS

To my family and Davide

INTRODUCTION

I've always loved plants. Growing up, I was inspired by my grandmas June and Rafaela, who were the quintessential plant ladies. Both sets of grandparents had large fruit and vegetable gardens at home, and I recall following them around the garden and assisting them with planting and harvesting as a child. I was too young to understand the science of what they were doing, but I was enamored nevertheless. As a young adult in New York City, I dreamed of filling my first apartment with a variety of interesting plants, but achieving that dream wasn't as simple as I'd hoped. I bought many plants only to then watch them die a slow and painful death—all due to my lack of plant knowledge and desire to buy plants based purely on appearance. I became frustrated and decided to learn as much as I could about plants and what makes them flourish. I read books, researched online, asked questions at the plant shops, bought more plants to practice with, and enrolled in plant-care classes at the Brooklyn Botanic Garden and *ta-da*! Here I stand, a plant lover who can't stop buying plants, talking about plants, learning about plants, and dreaming about plants. After a lot of diligence, education, and trial by error, I have been fortunate to be able turn my love of plants into a career as an interior plant designer who has the pleasure of selecting, styling, and caring for plants. With that comes educating new plant parents as well as expanding my own education.

The first two houseplants that I was able to keep alive were a peace lily I named Patsy (after Patsy Cline) and a small money tree I named Robert Plant (after, you guessed it, Robert Plant). I learned very quickly that Patsy was an emotional lady who would droop when she was thirsty but would perk back up an hour after having a big drink of water. When the foliage of Robert Plant was becoming discolored, I couldn't pinpoint the cause. But after some trial and error, I was able to find him a sweet spot in a window where he grew from a 1-foot-tall tree into an almost 7-foot-tall tree over the course of five years. Robert Plant has since moved on to the plant afterlife, proving that I will continue to make mistakes as a plant parent. And while the love and understanding that now goes into each of my plant relationships can be trying at times, at the end of the day, it's always immensely rewarding.

Beyond the ability of plants to bring beauty to your home, they also offer such benefits as filtering the air and inspiring creativity and focus. Overall, they improve the quality of your day-to-day life just by their sheer existence. They bring color, warmth, style, and life to a space. They really have a way of growing on you. Once you start surrounding yourself with plants, you won't be able to stop, because plants just make life better.

house planted

1

SOME FAVORITE PLANTS TO GET YOU STARTED

Because there are countless plants that come from all over the world, it can be difficult to choose which ones are right for you. While some are tricky to track down, there remain many wonderful varieties that are perfect for both novice and experienced plant parents. These species make great indoor plants, and, as long as you make an effort to re-create their natural habitats and get to know their personalities, cohabitation can be gratifying and lovely. Some plants may present various challenges in terms of their care requirements, but they'll keep you on your toes and continue to help you learn more about them—and maybe even learn more about yourself.

For each plant that follows, I provide a common name (for example, bird's nest fern) and the scientific name (for example, *Asplenium nidus*). Common names are like nicknames and can sometimes be shared by different plants, while each plant has only one scientific name. Although it's easier and more tempting to use the common name, I advise you check the scientific name when buying plants to make sure you don't accidentally end up getting a different plant than you intended. This is particularly true when buying plants online. Scientific names will also change or become updated from time to time as our knowledge grows.

If you're just getting started in the plant game, you'll have plenty of options for easy-care plants. If you're up for a challenge, look for plants that require a little more love. And, let's be honest, who *wouldn't* want a little more plant love?

Key: Difficulty   Light   Water   Toxicity

Bird of Paradise

Scientific Name: *Strelitzia reginae*

Though native to South Africa, this plant with shiny, boat-shaped leaves is found growing all over the world. Indoors, they make a statement as lush, oversized floor plants that, with ample light, can reach heights of 10 to 12 feet. Given the room to grow, they'll exceed that. In nature, their fanning leaves split naturally to allow strong winds to pass through without breaking the stalks. They also split indoors without the wind, but there's no cause for alarm as it's just their nature to do so. Their flowers resemble the colorful birds that the plant is named for, though they rarely bloom indoors. The bird of paradise is closely related to the banana plant and provides a great way to create a jungle feel in your home.

✂ Easy. Great for new plant parents.

☀ Bright direct sun is ideal, though it will tolerate lower to moderate light conditions.

💧 Fully saturate the soil, allowing the top 2 inches to dry out between each watering.

🍃 Toxic to cats and dogs.

Dragon Tree

Scientific Name: *Dracaena marginata*

Originally from Madagascar, the dragon tree will grow up to 20 feet tall in nature and about 10 feet indoors (but can go beyond, if given the space). The ribbon-like dark green foliage with burgundy edges has a lot of character and bursts from the tops of their stems like fireworks. As they grow, they shed lower, older leaves, which creates pretty diamond-shaped patterns on their stems. Their stems also offer up curvy growth habits, giving the dragon tree even more visual interest.

✂ Easy. Great for new plant parents.

☀ Best in bright indirect light, though tolerant of lower light conditions.

💧 Fully saturate the soil, allowing the top 2 inches to dry out between each watering. Reduce frequency of watering in colder months.

🍃 Toxic to cats and dogs.

Fiddle Leaf Fig

Scientific Name: *Ficus lyrata*

Native to Western Africa, the fiddle leaf fig has broad leaves and can grow to heights of 8 to 10 feet indoors and up to 25 feet outdoors. When given more room to grow indoors, they can exceed 10 feet. Consistent light and temperature are key to keeping these striking but fickle plants happy. When exposed to drastic changes in temperature or light, the fiddle leaf fig will rapidly shed its leaves. Its broad leaves collect dust pretty quickly, so put them in the tub for a shower or wipe down using a wet sponge from time to time—they'll welcome the humidity and the additional light that's able to get through (it will also wash off any existing pests).

✂ Advanced. Needs more love.

☀ Bright indirect, filtered light is best.

💧 Fully saturate the soil, allowing the top 2 inches to dry out between each watering. Reduce frequency of watering in colder months.

🍃 Toxic to cats and dogs.

Swiss Cheese Plant

Scientific Name: *Monstera deliciosa*

Native to Central America and the West Indies, the *Monstera deliciosa* is best known and identified by its oversized leaves with Swiss cheese–like holes. The holes help it withstand high winds in its natural, tropical habitat. In the wild, it will climb trees of great heights and completely cover tree trunks. Indoors, it makes an attractive, sprawling floor plant and, with the right support, an upright climbing plant. Smaller *Monstera* varieties are excellent hanging plants.

✄ Moderate. Not too needy.

☀ Moderate to bright indirect light is best. Long periods of direct sunlight will scorch the leaves, and, while it is tolerant of lower light conditions, this will significantly reduce the growth.

💧 Fully saturate the soil, allowing the top 2 inches to dry out between each watering. Reduce frequency of watering in colder months. The plant also enjoys some humidity or misting, but does just fine with the average humidity in the home.

🍃 Toxic to cats and dogs.

Congo Rojo Philodendron

Scientific Name: *Philodendron* 'Congo Rojo'

These philodendrons are native to Central and South America and have an upward, mound-like growth habit, unlike the more familiar trailing philodendrons. They have oversized, dark green leaves with deep burgundy stems and edges. New foliage is completely burgundy as it begins to emerge and unfurl, only turning green as it matures. They are visually very stunning with a tropical yet modern allure.

✄ Easy. Great for new plant parents.

☀ Bright indirect light is ideal, though the plant will tolerate moderate light conditions.

💧 Fully saturate the soil, allowing the top 2 inches to dry out between each watering. Reduce frequency of watering in colder months.

🍃 Toxic to cats and dogs. Sap is also a skin irritant. Wash thoroughly if your skin comes in contact with the sap.

Elephant's Ear

Scientific Name: *Alocasia* 'Regal Shields'

This is a stellar tropical plant with oversized, broad elephant ear–shaped, deep green foliage marked with light green veins. In the wild, the leaves will grow to enormous sizes of a few feet long, but indoors, they tend to range in size from 1 to 2 feet long and wide, depending on how much room they're given to grow. They produce spike-like white flowers, and while they are not showy, they are unique. Note that these plants are particularly prone to spider mites, so rinsing the foliage in the shower from time to time is recommended.

✄ Moderate. Not too needy.

☀ Bright indirect light is best, but the plant can acclimate to partial shade. Avoid direct sun.

💧 This humidity-loving plant loves moisture. Placement in a bathroom or misting on occasion is ideal. Fully saturate the soil, allowing the top 2 inches to dry out between each watering. Reduce frequency of watering in colder months.

🍃 Toxic to cats and dogs.

Peruvian Apple Cactus

Scientific Name: *Cereus repandus*

Native to South America, Peruvian apple cacti reach towering heights of more than 30 feet in the wild. Indoors they can grow to be about half that size, if they have the space and the right environment to do so. Their columns have deep indentations and are sometimes spiny along the ridges. In the right conditions, they will produce showy flowers that open for one night only, so be sure not to miss it.

✂ Easy. Great for new plant parents.

☀ Bright direct or indirect light is preferred, though the plant will tolerate partial shade.

💧 Fully saturate the soil and allow it to dry out completely between each watering. Reduce watering frequency by about half in colder months when the plant is dormant.

🍃 Nontoxic and pet-friendly.

Aloe Vera

Scientific Name: *Aloe vera*

Aloe vera originates from the Mediterranean and is sun-loving, yet easily adaptable to moderate light conditions indoors. They tend to grow a bit wild, with their arms reaching out toward the sunlight, which can make them quite beautiful and full of character. Aloes can reach heights of up to 3 feet, and their leaves can be almost 2 feet in length. Aloe vera is a great plant for removing toxins from the air, and its sap can be used to heal dry skin and burns. Though aloe vera will rarely bloom indoors, their flowers are a gorgeous orange color that tower high above the leaves.

✂ Easy. Great for new plant parents.

☀ Moderate to bright direct light is ideal.

💧 Fully saturate the soil and allow it to dry out completely between each watering. Reduce frequency of watering in colder months. Aloe is drought-tolerant, so when in doubt, less is more.

🍃 Toxic to cats, dogs, and humans if ingested.

Pencil Cactus

Scientific Name: *Euphorbia tirucalli*

Unusual in appearance, the pencil cactus resembles a bouquet of green pencils. There are also reddish pink–toned variegated varieties called sticks on fire (*Euphorbia tirucalli* 'Sticks on Fire'). Native to Africa, the pencil cactus can also be found in tropical climates and grows well as a houseplant. In nature, pencil cacti can grow to be very large, shrublike trees. Indoors, they'll grow as big as you allow them, depending on the size of the pot and amount of light they're getting. They typically have small leaves on stalks that tend to be shed during their dormancy period in the colder months.

✂ Easy. Great for new plant parents.

☀ Bright light is best, but the plant can tolerate medium light conditions.

💧 Fully saturate the soil and allow it to dry out completely between each watering. Reduce frequency of watering in colder months

🍃 Toxic to cats and dogs. It also produces a white, milky sap that can irritate the skin. Wash thoroughly if your skin comes in contact with the sap.

Variegated Wax Plant

Scientific Name: *Hoya carnosa* 'Variegata'

The wax plant is native to tropical regions in the Pacific Islands and Australia and is an epiphyte that can be found growing up and trailing down trees (an epiphyte grows on the surface of plants but is not parasitic). This variety has thick, green, waxy leaves with hints of pink and cream tones. The leaves cascade down long vines and produce cute little waxy flower clusters that are extremely fragrant. If you look closely, you'll see up to fifty flowers in one cluster. They do enjoy being a little root-bound, so don't rush to repot if it's happy and thriving.

✂ Moderate. Not too needy.

☀ Moderate to bright indirect light is best.

💧 Fully saturate the soil and allow it to dry out almost completely between each watering. Avoid overwatering as the wax plants do not like wet feet and require a well-draining soil and planter. Reduce watering by about half during colder months.

🍃 Nontoxic and pet-friendly.

String of Pearls

Scientific Name: *Curio rowleyanus*

Originating in South Africa, the string of pearls is a succulent that stores water in its pealike leaves. As an indoor plant, with well-draining soil and planter, it will thrive beautifully and, in the warmer months, may even produce pretty white-pink pom-pom flowers that are fragrant and smell of cinnamon. While the fragrance may not perme-ate the room, the plant smells lovely up close. String of pearls prefers to be sun-facing, and if you're able to provide some top-down sunlight via a skylight, it will remain full at the top and trail beautifully to make a daz-zling hanging plant.

✂ Advanced. Needs more love.

☀ Bright indirect light is ideal; too much intense light will likely dry out the pearls.

💧 Fully saturate the soil and allow it to dry out completely between each watering. Reduce watering by about half in colder months. This plant can with-stand drought and infrequent watering.

🍃 Toxic to cats and dogs.

Hindu Rope Hoya

Scientific Name: *Hoya carnosa* 'Compacta'

Native to East Asia, this epiphytic vine has very thick, tightly ruffled, twisting leaves that dangle like ropes. They produce star-shaped clusters of fragrant pink flowers that are waxy just like the leaves. These plants are drought-tolerant and do not like wet feet, so a well-draining porous pot and potting mix are ideal.

✂ Moderate. Not too needy.

☀ Bright indirect, diffused light is best.

💧 Fully saturate the soil, allowing the top 2 inches to dry out between each watering. Leaves will begin to pucker when thirsty. Reduce frequency of watering in colder months.

🍃 Nontoxic and pet-friendly.

Satin Pothos

Scientific Name: *Scindapsus pictus* 'Argyraeus'

The silvery blue-gray foliage of the satin pothos lives up to its name with its soft, satin-like texture. Its foliage is robust and thick, protecting the plant from intense sunlight. In its native home of Southeast Asia, the plant climbs up trees using aerial roots to secure itself. As it grows up the trunks of trees, the leaves will shingle or flatten out against the surface. Indoors, this plant will trail beautifully from a shelf or hanging planter, and it can also grow upward, affixing itself to the wall in the right growing conditions. The satin pothos is alternatively known as the silver philodendron, but it is neither a true pothos nor a philodendron.

✂ Easy. Great for new plant parents.

☀ This plant does well in a range of light, from low to bright. Bright direct light may cause some leaf stress.

💧 Fully saturate the soil, allowing the top 2 inches to dry out between each watering. Reduce frequency of watering in colder months.

🍃 Toxic to cats and dogs.

Spider Plant

Scientific Name: *Chlorophytum comosum*

Native to southern and tropical Africa, the spider plant is one of the most popular house-plants around the world. It is easy to grow, and the plantlets it produces resemble spiders cascading downward, up to a few feet in length, making it a great plant for a hanging planter or shelf. With optimal growing conditions, the plant will grow rapidly. When happy, a spider plant produces small white flowers that eventually flourish into plantlets—and often those plantlets produce plantlets, too! The spider plant also has amazing air-purifying qualities, rendering it an excellent choice for city dwellers.

✂ Easy. Great for new plant parents.

☀ Bright indirect light is ideal, though it tolerates moderate light conditions.

💧 Fully saturate the soil, allowing the top 2 inches to dry out between each watering. If not, know that they are somewhat drought-tolerant and tend to bounce back if they become a little overly thirsty. Reduce frequency of watering in colder months.

🍃 Nontoxic and pet-friendly.

Velvet Leaf Philodendron

Scientific Name: *Philodendron hederaceum* var. *hederaceum*

These philodendrons (often synonymously called *P. micans* and *P. scandens*) come from lush, temperate climates in the Americas, though they are found all around the world. Their heart-shaped, iridescent foliage is a deep shade of green with rich purple undersides and a velvety texture. They trail beautifully and will also climb upward with the right support. Easy to propagate, they're also great as clippings in vases around the home or to share with friends and family.

✂ Easy. Great for new plant parents.

☀ Low to bright filtered light is best.

💧 Fully saturate the soil, allowing the top 2 inches to dry out between each watering. Reduce frequency of watering in colder months. Wilting, limp foliage is often a sign of thirst, but once watered, the foliage will spring back.

🍃 Toxic to cats and dogs.

Bird's Nest Anthurium

Scientific Name: *Anthurium plowmanii*

The bird's nest anthurium is native to South America and grows epiphytically, meaning that in its natural habitat, it grows on other plants or trees. Their thick, wavy, semi-succulent leaves can grow to be about 6 feet in length, and they have a growth habit similar to that of the bird's nest fern (page 25). These resilient plants look as though they might have been plucked from a prehistoric landscape and always make me think to myself, "Life finds a way."

✂ Easy. Great for new plant parents.

☀ Moderate to bright indirect light is best, but it will tolerate somewhat lower light conditions.

💧 Fully saturate the soil, allowing the top 2 inches to dry out between each watering. While this plant is drought-tolerant, it does enjoy a good drink of water in well-draining soil. Reduce frequency of watering in colder months.

🌿 Toxic to cats and dogs.

Rubber Plant

Scientific Name: *Ficus elastica* 'Variegata'

Originating from the Himalayas, the variegated rubber plant has robust, painterly, light green foliage with creamy edges. Indoors, they'll likely grow to be 5 to 8 feet tall and begin to branch out as they do in their natural habitat. As with many houseplants, given the space, they'll surpass that height. Outdoor specimens grow to be 50 to 100 feet tall. Dusting their leaves regularly is recommended to keep them shiny, pest-free, and capable of getting plenty of sunlight.

✂ Easy. Great for new plant parents.

☀ Moderate to bright indirect light is ideal.

💧 Fully saturate the soil, allowing the top 2 inches to dry out between each watering. Reduce frequency of watering in colder months.

🌿 Toxic to cats and dogs. The sticky white sap can irritate skin, so be sure to wash if you come in contact with it.

Cast Iron Plant

Scientific Name: *Aspidistra elatior*

The cast iron plant is native to Asia and is found growing in abundance in the forest understory. They can grow to be about 3 feet tall and have long, arching, deep green leaves that are structured but not rigid. They also have parallel veins that give the leaves a subtly ribbed texture. They benefit from regular dusting because their large leaves collect dust easily. These plants are extremely manageable, hard to kill, and regal in appearance.

✂ Easy. Great for new plant parents.

☀ Lower light conditions are ideal. Bright, direct sun will burn the leaves.

💧 Fully saturate the soil, allowing the top 2 inches to dry out between each watering. Reduce frequency of watering in colder months.

🌿 Nontoxic and pet-friendly.

Ponytail Palm

Scientific Name: *Beaucarnea recurvata*

Native to Mexico, these beauties will grow up to 30 feet tall in the wild and up to about 8 feet tall indoors. That said, they are typically small when purchased from nurseries or plant shops. They are not true palms but rather belong to the same family as the snake plant (at right), Asparagaceae. Ponytail palms store water in their rotund, bottle-like trunks, so it's best to err on the side of giving them less water rather than more. If you're lucky enough to see your ponytail flower, you're in for a stunner. They produce a burst of soft yellow flowers that tower over the green foliage and resemble pampas grass. Flowering typically occurs on very mature and large specimens. It has been known to take up to 30 years to flower indoors, and it would certainly be worth the wait.

🪰 Easy. Great for new plant parents.

☀️ Bright direct light is ideal.

💧 Fully saturate the soil, allowing the top 2 inches to dry out between each watering. Reduce frequency of watering in colder months.

🐾 Nontoxic and pet-friendly.

Snake Plant

Scientific Name: *Dracaena trifasciata* (formerly *Sansevieria trifasciata*)

Snake plants are native to West Africa, where they thrive in warm, tropical climates. As houseplants, they adapt well to a wide range of growing conditions, making them extremely low maintenance and ideal for the novice plant owner. Their foliage is thick, sturdy, and shaped like spears. Though they rarely flower as houseplants, their small white flowers smell like carnations, and the fragrance will permeate a room. Snake plants are available in a plethora of varieties, ranging in color and striations and can grow to be about 5 feet tall.

🪰 Easy. Great for new plant parents.

☀️ Tolerant of low light, but it thrives in brighter light conditions.

💧 A very sporadic watering schedule is best—ideally once every 2 to 3 weeks, when the soil is completely dry. Fully saturate the soil and discard any water that has collected in the saucer to avoid root rot.

🐾 Toxic to cats and dogs.

ZZ Plant

Scientific Name: *Zamioculcas zamiifolia*

These plants are native to South and East Africa, where they thrive in warm tropical climates. Indoors, they can withstand a little neglect, and their rich green foliage splays beautifully. While they do well in lower light conditions, with brighter light, they'll send out lots of new growth. When emerging, the foliage looks like stalks of asparagus until the leaves begin to reveal themselves.

🪰 Easy. Great for new plant parents.

☀️ The zz does well in a wide range of lighting. Just be sure it's getting some sunlight to maintain and more to really thrive.

💧 Fully saturate the soil and allow it to dry out almost completely between each watering. This plant is drought-tolerant and can adapt to your watering schedule, provided you're not overwatering at any point. Reduce frequency of watering in colder months.

🐾 Toxic to cats and dogs.

Fishbone Cactus

Scientific Name: *Epiphyllum anguliger*

This striking cactus is native to Mexico, where it is found growing on tree trunks. Its deeply serrated, zigzagging stems resemble fishbones (hence, its common name). They are a jungle cactus with arching foliage and produce beautiful yellow and white, mildly fragrant flowers that only bloom for one day.

Moderate. Not too needy.

Bright indirect light is best, though the plant will acclimate to slightly lower light conditions. Avoid direct sunlight.

Fully saturate the soil, allowing the top 2 inches to dry out between each watering. Reduce frequency of watering in colder months. They also like a little bit more humidity than other cacti but do just fine in any room in your home and don't require frequent misting.

Nontoxic and pet-friendly.

Chinese Money Plant

Scientific Name: *Pilea peperomioides*

The Chinese money plant, also called the friendship plant, is native to China. It spreads via underground stems called rhizomes and produces pilea pups (offshoots) that make it easy to propagate and share with others. The foliage is semi-succulent, so it does not like to be overwatered or surrounded by a lot of humidity. Rotate its pot regularly if you prefer a symmetrical plant shape. If you like a plant that's a little more wild and unusual in shape, let it get comfy in one spot, and it will stretch out and do its own thing.

Moderate. Not too needy.

Bright indirect light is best, but the plant will tolerate moderate light conditions. If the light is too intense, the edges of the leaves will become reddish in tone.

Fully saturate the soil and allow it to dry out almost completely between each watering. Reduce frequency of watering in colder months.

Nontoxic and pet-friendly.

Red Mistletoe Cactus

Scientific Name: *Pseudorhipsalis ramulosa*

Native to Central and South America, the red mistletoe cactus is an epiphytic jungle cactus that grows in trees. It has long, flat, ribbon-like leaves with twiggy stems that drape, making it an ideal plant for a shelf or a hanging planter. It also produces small mistletoe-like berries, and the foliage will turn an outstanding, jaw-dropping reddish purple in brighter light conditions.

Easy. Great for new plant parents.

Partial sun is ideal, but the more light it receives, the deeper the reddish-purple tones will be. Be careful not to scorch the leaves with too much direct sunlight.

Don't let the cactus name fool you—this one likes regular watering. Fully saturate the soil and allow it to dry out almost completely between each watering. A little humidity from misting or a bathroom is also welcome, though not imperative.

Nontoxic and pet-friendly.

Staghorn Fern

Scientific Name: *Platycerium bifurcatum*

Staghorn ferns are native to Southeast Asia, Polynesia, and Australia and are epiphytic plants. Their fronds can grow to lengths of about 3 feet. The brown fronds near the base produce spores that allow the plant to reproduce. The other fronds at the base of the plant are known as shield fronds, and they protect the roots of the plant. Staghorn ferns can be mounted onto wood slabs or grown in pots. If grown in pots, you'll want to be sure it is in a sphagnum fern mix for best results.

Moderate. Not too needy.

Bright indirect light is best; be sure not to expose it to direct sunlight.

If potted, fully saturate the soil, allowing the top 2 inches to dry out between each watering. Discard excess water in saucer. Mounted ferns should be submerged in water so only the root ball is soaked for about 15 minutes every 7 to 10 days in warmer months. Allow the plant to drip-dry before rehanging. Mist the fronds regularly. Reduce frequency of watering in colder months.

Nontoxic and pet-friendly.

Bird's Nest Fern

Scientific Name: *Asplenium nidus*

The bird's nest fern is native to tropical climates, such as Hawaii, Australia, and Southeast Asia. In their natural habitat, they can grow up to 3 feet wide and 5 feet tall, but most houseplant specimens are more contained and smaller in their indoor environment. Their bright green, undulating fronds unfurl from a central rosette and splay outward. In nature, the fern grows epiphytically on trees and collects fallen leaves that decompose in the central rosette to provide the plant with additional nutrients.

Moderate. Not too needy.

Moderately bright light is preferred. Avoid direct sun.

Fully saturate the soil around the base of the plant when the soil is almost dry. Avoid watering directly into the center rosette, because this could cause the plant to rot. Reduce frequency of watering in colder months.

Nontoxic and pet-friendly.

Polka Dot Begonia

Scientific Name: *Begonia maculata*

Native to South America, begonias are great houseplants with showy angel wing–shaped leaves. Their foliage is silver spotted on top with a burgundy underbelly, and they have a bushy growth habit, reaching heights of up to 5 feet. Be sure to keep them away from cold, drafty windows and out of direct, intense sunlight. If you're lucky, they will produce pretty white flowers in the late winter and spring.

Moderate. Not too needy.

Best in moderate, indirect light. They can adjust to bright direct light conditions; however, the foliage may get a little brassy.

Fully saturate the soil, allowing the top 2 inches to dry out between each watering. They can withstand periods of dryness, though they thrive in humid conditions such as bathrooms. Reduce frequency of watering in colder months.

Toxic to cats and dogs.

2

PLANTS IN EVERY ROOM

Bringing plants into the home allows city dwellers and those of us without an outdoor space to easily inject some nature into our everyday lives. Tropical plants, cacti, and succulents inspire daydreams of warmer climates during colder months and remind us year-round that nature is ever present. Greenery breathes life into a space, helping to create a cozy, welcoming environment. And while a plant or two can certainly make a room feel more alive, a mix of several plants, thoughtfully arranged, can transform any space into a stylish oasis.

Before acquiring plants for your home, there are a few important things to consider. Are there empty corners, bookshelves, windowsills, or tabletops that could benefit from plant life? Thinking ahead just a bit, will there be ample room for your plants to mature and grow into the space? Do you want your space to be minimally enhanced by plants, or do you want it to feel lush with plant life? Once you have some of those questions answered, you can take the next steps of identifying which plants you like and determining whether they'll be a good fit for your home.

Consider how much time you'll be able to dedicate to your plants on a weekly basis, as well as the amount of light you have in your space. If you travel frequently or work long hours, introducing low-maintenance plants like cacti or succulents (in bright-light spaces) or cast iron plants (in low-light spaces) are great options. If you're home consistently and are up for more hands-on plant parenting, you can select plants that need more attention, like ferns. As long as you ensure that your plants will get enough light, water, and TLC to thrive, you'll be set. Plus, your plants will always let you know if they're unhappy. Keep an eye on them and adjust as needed while you acclimate to each other. You get to create your own indoor plant haven, so have fun and don't be afraid to make mistakes. Get inspired and bring on the plants.

Bedroom Greens

The bedroom is a place of retreat and relaxation. It's where you unwind; it's your private space for resting and recharging. Plants can enhance that sense of calm after a long day. Plants that purify the air, like snake plants or spider plants, placed on your nightstands or around your bed, will guarantee a better night's rest. If your bedroom has bright light, try a flowering plant like lavender or jasmine to reduce stress with their sweet fragrances. If you have a big window, adding hanging plants or plants on the windowsill will provide some privacy and help to reduce outside sounds. It's also just wonderful to wake up and fall asleep among plants in your bedroom, so don't hold back from making your bedroom lush, vibrant, and full of life. It's totally worth it.

Hanging planters showcase
beautiful cascading foliage.
Cultivate sweet dreams by
hanging plants in the bedroom.

Give an oversized plant
the shine it deserves
in a bright window. Who
needs curtains when
you have plants?

Kitchen Greens

The kitchen is a perfect place to add freshness with plants. If your kitchen gets bright light, try growing some herbs such as mint, basil, or thyme. Growing edible plants in your kitchen makes it easy to have access to fresh herbs, veggies, or fruits for cooking, though kitchen plants don't have to be edible. If you don't have the space in the window, the top of the fridge, the countertop, or on an open shelf will work for potted plants. Keep in mind that the top of the fridge will likely emit more heat to the base of the plant than a shelf would, which may mean you'll need to water a bit more frequently. A plant with a more vertical growth habit, like a zz plant or a small rubber plant, atop the fridge is a good option to avoid any foliage getting in the way of opening the refrigerator door. A shelf in the kitchen is a great place for a slow-growing, trailing plant like a wax plant, fishbone cactus, or red mistletoe cactus. If you have the space on your countertop, try a grouping of plants in a corner. Plants in the kitchen will also purify the air and help with productivity, particularly if you're an avid cook.

Plants in a window help bring some of the outside greenery in.

Greens in the kitchen don't always have to be in a salad bowl.

Small accents on the dining table with larger plants on the floor create warmth and variety. Keep the plants on the table small so people can see over them while eating.

A plant near the sink is easy to water, plus a windowsill is a great spot for a lush trailing plant—you can either prune as often as you'd like or let it go wild.

Bathroom Greens

The bathroom is the place where we spend time gearing up for the day, and if your bathroom has natural sunlight, it's an excellent place to add some greenery. Studies have shown that plants can encourage us, motivate us, and reduce our stress levels, so bringing them into the bathroom can help you start your day on the right foot.

Humidity-loving plants, such as ferns and begonias, which can sometimes be tough to keep happy in drier spots in your space, feel right at home in the bathroom. The moisture from your daily shower will save you from having to spritz them with water, and they will thrive happily. Other air-purifying plants such as spider plants or snake plants will serve a more practical purpose by removing toxins and keep your bathroom fresh and clean.

*Greens in green:
Shades of green plants in
green pots are always a
welcome sight and add
a splash of color and life
to a bathroom.*

*Delicate meets exuberant
with this air-purifying
dynamic duo.*

Living Room Greens

In the living room, plants can provide visual character in a way furniture alone cannot. Plants add shape and color and make the space feel cozy and lived in. If you have a big window or an empty corner, try adding an oversized plant like a Swiss cheese plant or an elephant's ear as a statement piece and focal point in the room. Such large plants draw the eye and bring drama to a space. Similarly, larger tropical plants such as a bird of paradise and the fiddle leaf fig bring instant warmth and lushness. If you have the space for it, grouping plants of varying heights, colors, and/or textures together adds visual interest. Plants on the coffee or side table are long-lasting solutions in place of fresh-cut flowers and provide an accent of green that makes the space all the more inviting.

It's scientifically proven that plants grow faster under and behind glass. If you haven't got the space on the floor or tabletop, try filling your windows with sun-loving plants such as aloe vera, a pencil cactus, or a rubber plant. But be aware of those drafty windows in winter and the scorching sun in summer. If your windows are drafty, you may want to consider moving your plants a few feet away from the window in the colder months. With intensified sunshine in the warmer months, you'll likely need to increase the watering frequency.

Take a vacant corner of the living room and add plants at varying heights to transform an empty space into a focal point.

Add a trailing plant to bring some wildness to a structured environment.

*Plants are nature's artwork.
Why not throw a piece up
on the wall?*

*Classic terra-cotta pots add
warmth and simplicity that
cozy up the room.*

Office Greens

Studies have shown that having plants in an office space can increase focus, productivity, and creativity; reduce stress; and improve your mood. Plants help warm up aesthetically sterile offices, regulate humidity, and remove harmful toxins from the air; according to NASA studies, they can even help prevent sickness. Plants clear the air and the mind. More is more when it comes to having plants in your workspace, because the benefits of having them around are fulfilling on so many levels. Plants at your desk also allow you to personalize your space.

While many offices may not have the best natural sunlight, there are still plenty of low-light plants to choose from. My go-to low-light and low-maintenance plants are the snake plant and zz plant. Their vertical growth structures also help keep your desktop clear for office supplies (though I would certainly argue that plants are essential office supplies!).

3

PLANT STYLING

While there is no one specific recipe for plant styling, there are some basic guidelines to help you get started. The most important thing to remember is that whatever you do should reflect your personal style. Don't be afraid to try a few variations on plants, planters, and their placement before settling on the ideal arrangement that works best for you. Look for inspiration around you. There is so much information, knowledge, and creativity out there. As long as you're mindful of the care requirements for each of your plants, you can even try sitting with a few different setups to see how they feel. Perhaps you have a plant that you thought might be great in a certain location but come to find that it's blocking the walkway a little bit, or it isn't having the impact that you were hoping for. It's all about trial and error, so don't let that hold you back from adjusting as you see fit.

Houseplants come in a seemingly countless array of shapes, textures, colors, and sizes, so there truly is something to fit every home's look and feel. Try to mix and match plants that have more structure and rigid lines with free-flowing plants that are more wild and lush. You can vary planter shapes, colors, and styles as well as plants of different textures, heights, and colors to achieve different looks. The possibilities are endless, and it's up to you to decide what works best in your space. Embrace the process!

Planters

While selecting plants may seem like the primary focus when considering your indoor garden, planters also play an important role. They house the root systems of your plants and make a design statement that can transform your space.

Planters come in all shapes, colors, and sizes, and can be made of materials such as terra-cotta, glazed ceramic, plastic, or metal. These varying planter materials should be considered along with your plant's watering needs, as some planters are more porous and allow the soil to dry faster, whereas other materials hold in the moisture. In an ideal world, all planters would have drainage holes and accompanying saucers to promote happy, healthy roots. But don't worry; there are solutions to keeping plants in planters without drainage holes. You can also repurpose other containers such as baskets or tins to serve as planters (just remember to poke a few holes in the bottom, or if you can't, see the potting instructions on page 81). When it comes to planter size, select a planter that is about 2 inches deeper and wider than your plant's nursery pot.

If you prefer a clean aesthetic, try using planters that are all the same color or even varying shades within the same color family. If you're feeling more adventurous, try an eclectic mix of planter colors, shapes, and textures. If you're somewhere in the middle, you can select planters with similar shapes and vary the colors, sizes, and textures a bit. You could also try keeping the bulk of your planters consistent in color and texture, but sprinkle in a planter or two that are completely different for a subtle pop. It's really about your personal style, but if you're ever in doubt, keep it classic with terra-cotta pots. You can always upgrade from there.

house planted

Plant Stands

Plant stands give your plants a boost in height and get them up off the floor. That extra lift can be great if you have a plant on the floor that needs to be closer to the window for added sunlight. If you have pets or kids, plant stands help keep plants out of reach (be careful that your stand isn't too top heavy or easily knocked over, though). They also add a nice layered look if you have a plant group on the floor and allow you to display the planter and plant more distinctly and openly. A single plant stand can also be a great stand-alone piece—particularly if you have a unique or vintage plant stand. You can find stands made to hold plants at home and garden stores, but you can also employ household items as stands, such as small side tables, stools, benches, ladders, or even stacks of books. Be mindful of water drainage and use a cork platter or glazed saucer between your pot and the makeshift plant stand to protect against potential water damage. Another option for giving a plant some extra lift is to place its pot on top of another planter turned upside down. I find this works particularly well with terra-cotta pots.

Plant Groupings

Grouping plants together is a way to easily warm up a space and make it feel lush, even if your assortment of plants is modest. It's best to group plants that have similar light requirements, and, while it's not as necessary, grouping plants with similar watering needs will help keep things simple come watering time. Plants with similar watering needs will also assist each other with added humidity. Grouping plants in odd numbers creates visual interest and balance, and grouping them in varying heights adds texture and fullness to a space, whether it's on the floor, a tabletop, or a shelf. Corners or nooks are often ideal places for grouping plants together and can be functional without it feeling like the space is being overrun by greenery.

You can also group a variety of different plants into a single planter or group one variety of plant in multiple planters. If you want to group different plants into a single planter, choose ones that have the same light and watering needs, since you won't have control over how much water goes to the roots of each plant. Also consider their root systems and how quickly they might grow or interact with each other as they mature.

Room Divider

Plants can provide privacy and help break up an open space by creating a breathable wall. Try topping a console table or bench with a row of vertical plants such as snake plants to create a room divider, or establish a dividing wall of palms potted in a long rectangular planter on the floor. If you're not a fan of a single rectangular planter, try grouping a few rounded planters together in a row. These will help break up the space without completely closing it off and will allow nice filtered air to flow through. Alternatively, try using an open bookcase as a room divider and filling it with lush trailing plants. The shelves allow trailing plants to cascade downward, highlighting their foliage, and make a breathable wall. Try mixing in nontrailing plants and nonplant items for some variation as well.

Living on the Wall

If you don't have the space for potted plants on a tabletop or the floor, mounting plants on the wall is another way to create a vibrant green focal point. It can also serve as a living art piece without taking up space elsewhere. There are specially made planters that lie flat against the wall that you can source. Most may not have drainage holes, and if that is so, see the potting instructions on page 81 to prevent rotting roots. In addition to safely securing the planter to the wall, you'll want to consider the light and watering needs of the plants, as well as the weight of the plants, since freshly watered plants can be quite heavy. Alternatively, you can also find epiphytic plants such as staghorn ferns or wax plants mounted on wood slabs that can be hung easily with some wire and a single nail or screw. Because these plants naturally grow on trees, the wood slabs closely resemble their native habitat. This is my favorite lightweight option for wall-mounted plants. Should you go this route, consider the ease and frequency of removing the plant for watering, as well as the drying time it'll require before you return it to the wall—this will help you avoid water damage on the wall itself.

Plant Shelf

Shelves are such a great way to display plants and utilize vertical space if you don't have the room on the floor, windowsill, or tabletop. If you have ample room, this is where you can add an abundance of plants grouped together in various planter sizes, along with a wide variety of plants. Even if you're a minimalist when it comes to design, this could be an opportunity to maximize with greenery in a concentrated area. Experiment with varying trailing plants, such as a velvet leaf philodendron, a red mistletoe cactus, or a satin pothos, and combine them with upright plants, such as a ponytail palm or an elephant's ear for texture and variation. As before, be sure to group plants with similar light needs together, and consider the weight of the plants post-watering if the shelf is wall-mounted.

Air Plant Display

Air plants are a type of epiphyte that do not require soil or a planter but rather get their nutrients from the air, rain, and wind in nature. As indoor plants, they require weekly 15-minute-long warm water baths (ideally in distilled water) and benefit from spraying with a foliar fertilizer for nutrients once a month. It's extremely important to shake off the excess water post-bath, rest upside down, and allow them to dry completely to avoid rot. When styling, air plants can be placed on a shelf or tabletop as stand-alone pieces and can be easily moved around your space given they receive the right amount of light. If you're feeling adventurous, you can mount them on a wall or onto a frame to display them. There is a plethora of air plant–specific hangers that can be secured to the wall. Styles range from malleable clawlike wall mounts that grasp the air plant securely by the base or wire-strung frames to which you can affix a number of air plants. As long as your air plants can be removed easily for soaking, an air plant wall display is an easy and impactful way to incorporate plants into your home.

Hanging Plants

Hanging plants are a nice way to mix up the presentation of greenery in the home. They draw the eye to a different level, which adds a nice variation and interest to the space. Hanging plants can be used to create privacy in a window and are a great way to get plants into a space with limited surfaces on which to place them. Plants can be hung using specialty hanging planters with cords and a hook attached, or with macrame or fabric plant hangers that can hold many styles of planters such as classic terra-cotta pots. Trailing plants like golden pothos, heartleaf philodendrons, string of pearls, spider plants, and wax plants are especially good candidates for hanging. Always make sure to leave an inch or two of space between the top of the soil and the lip of the pot to avoid water overflow and drips, and ensure that your ceiling can bear the weight of the pot, soil, plant, and water—they can get heavy! If your planter does not have a drainage hole, see the potting instructions on page 81 to maintain healthy roots.

4

PLANT SELECTION AND CARE

Selecting the right plants for your space begins with analyzing the layout and design of your home, the temperature and available light, as well as your lifestyle and plant knowledge. Choosing plants that look great and are manageable to maintain will enhance your enjoyment of them and ensure they stay healthy and robust. Start by considering what sizes, shapes, colors, and textures of plants (and planters) you're drawn to, then look around your space for empty spots that might be enhanced with plants. Empty surfaces can be excellent places to introduce plants, and if you're short on surfaces, you can always think vertically and incorporate hanging plants. A little greenery goes a long way and will elevate the overall look and feel of a space.

Once you have a sense of your design preferences and available locations around your home or office, you can figure out which plants will realistically work for your space and lifestyle. A common mistake is buying a plant for its visual appeal without having the understanding of its environmental needs, and the result is often the death of a new plant. Avoid that unfortunate scenario by getting a handle on how much available light there is in all the spots you hope to add greenery to (see page 89 for more on light) and by being honest about how much maintenance you can handle.

Once you've decided in which areas of your space you'd like to incorporate plants, you're ready to hit the nursery to hunt for the best specimens. Start by examining a plant's leaves. Firm, green leaves are a sign of a plant's health. If the leaves feel or look limp, consider selecting a different plant. Note that some plants have a drooping growth habit, so don't be afraid to ask the nursery or shop attendant to tell you about the plant in order to help you gain an understanding of its characteristics and personality. Always avoid yellowing, browning, and black leaves, as well as leaf spots or any other signs that the plant might be stressed. One discolored leaf shouldn't be something that deters you from adopting a new plant, but if you see that many of the leaves are discolored, move on. Keep an eye out for noticeable pests. While most pests are hard to see, some, such as fuzzy white mealy bugs or webbing from spider mites, reveal themselves clearly. Finally, it's always best to buy plants from a reputable plant nursery or shop where the plants have room to breathe and receive natural sunlight—there's where you're most likely to find happy, healthy plants.

Common Toxic Plants

While houseplants enhance our lives and homes in so many ways, some do have a low level of toxicity, such as dumb cane (*Dieffenbachia*) and peace lilies (*Spathiphyllum*), that can be dangerous to pets and humans. Some have sap that can irritate your skin, while others will cause nausea or oral irritation if ingested by pets or humans. Therefore, toxicity is something to keep in mind when selecting plants for your home. It's important to realize, though, that toxic does not necessarily mean fatal—most toxic houseplants will give you or your pet an upset stomach for a short period. To avoid any unpleasant situations, it is good to be aware of which houseplants are not recommended should you have pets or children that take a particular interest in plants. Try keeping the plants out of reach if you're at all concerned that the children or the pets may attempt to ingest them. The plant profiles on pages 9–25 list the toxicity level for each plant.

Potting Plants

Knowing how to pot a plant properly is a key skill for a successful plant parent. When you bring home a new plant, you'll want to transfer it from its temporary plastic pot into a more permanent home with room to grow. Some plants, however, are overly sensitive to environmental change, including the polka dot begonia and fiddle leaf fig. The sudden change in environment alone may cause them to drop some of their foliage, so give them a week or two to acclimate in their plastic nursery pots before repotting. This will help reduce the shock to their systems.

You'll also want to consider repotting your existing plants from time to time—it's a beneficial task to do once every year or two in order to maintain their health. You'll know it's time to repot if your plant is overgrown or top-heavy, if it has hit a plateau in terms of new growth, if the soil doesn't appear to take up or hold water, or if its roots are growing out of the base or up and out the top of the planter. Plants need a little time to acclimate to their new homes, and there may be a dip in their health as they're adjusting. As long as you establish a steady watering routine and consistent light and temperature, they'll settle in nicely.

Potting materials and tools:

- Worktable
- Newspaper (optional)
- Planter and saucer
- Small rocks, pebbles, or reused Styrofoam packing peanuts (only for pots without drainage holes)
- Horticultural charcoal (only for pots without drainage holes)
- Fresh potting soil
- Scoop for soil (if potting a plant that's still in its plastic nursery pot, you can use that)
- Watering can
- Plant
- Scissors or pruners
- Spray bottle filled with water

Potting Instructions

1 Set up your materials on a worktable or counter with an easy-to-clean surface. If you are concerned about getting dirt on your surface, put down a layer of newspaper.

2 Select a planter with a drainage hole and saucer. If the vessel does not have a drainage hole, you can create your own form of drainage (see step 3), but a planter with a drainage hole is preferred. Planter size is important. Cacti and succulents prefer tighter living quarters, as their roots tend to be shorter. When potting a cactus or succulent, choose a planter that's approximately 1 to 2 inches deeper and wider than the plastic container it came in. When potting a foliage plant, choose a planter that's approximately 2 to 3 inches deeper and wider to accommodate their more substantial root system.

house planted

3 If your planter has a drainage hole, skip to step 4. If, and only if, your planter does not have a drainage hole, place a 1- or 2-inch layer of rocks, pebbles, or used (nonbiodegradable) Styrofoam packing peanuts at the bottom of the pot. This is a great opportunity to reuse Styrofoam packing peanuts that you may have received in a shipment. On top of that, place a thin layer of horticultural charcoal. Horticultural charcoal helps to absorb impurities in the soil and also protects against overwatering.

4 Select potting soil appropriate for the plant type. Cacti and succulents like soil that's a bit sandy (think desert), allowing for better drainage, while foliage plants prefer a potting mix that retains moisture longer. Check that the soil is lightly moist before potting, adding water if needed.

5 If you're using a planter with a drainage hole, layer a couple inches of potting soil at the bottom of the planter and gently compress the soil. The idea is to avoid having the soil so loose that the water runs straight through but not so tightly compressed that the water can't get through to the roots. If you're potting into a planter without a drainage hole, place this layer of soil on top of the rocks, pebbles, or Styrofoam and horticultural charcoal.

6 Remove the plant from its plastic container by gently squeezing around the sides to loosen the plant and soil within the container. If you're transplanting from a nonplastic pot, it's best to allow wet soil to become slightly moist or dry for ease of removal and transfer. Take a look at the roots: Are they tightly wound around the plant or do they appear comfortable and not overcrowded? If tightly wound, take some time to loosen, just as you would comb hair to remove tangles, in this case being careful not to damage the roots. Using a clean pair of scissors or pruners, remove roots that appear to be black and/or mushy and remove some of the existing soil as well. The removal of some of the existing soil from the root ball allows you to introduce additional fresh potting soil and thus fresh nutrients.

7 Carefully place the plant in the center of the planter. You'll want the top of the plant's soil and root ball to be roughly 2 to 3 inches below the rim of the planter. Note that this will vary based on the size of your planter. The goal is to provide ample space to cover the root ball completely and evenly, while giving the plant's roots room to grow at the base. If the plant is sitting too low in the planter, add some more soil to the base layer at the bottom of the pot. Alternatively, if it's sitting too high, you'll need to remove a little bit of the soil at the bottom.

house planted

8 Fill the surrounding area with potting soil and add a top layer of at least 1 inch, while leaving 1 to 2 inches of space from the soil to the top of the planter. This keeps the water from overflowing from the top of the planter when watering. As before with the bottom layer of soil, gently press the soil down and around within the planter, being mindful to apply a moderate amount of pressure.

9 Water your plant and, if needed, clean the foliage by spritzing it with water. This helps your plant settle into its new home.

10 Place your plant in a spot that will allow it to get the light and comfortable temperature it needs to thrive.

Plant Cuttings and Propagation

Plant cuttings are a nice way to display plants as you would cut flowers, but with more longevity and very little maintenance. Cuttings also allow you to propagate new baby plants, granting you an opportunity to grow your plant collection for free. Cuttings also make nice gifts that you can give to and exchange with friends. Not all cuttings will root, but it is incredibly fascinating and rewarding to watch the growth process of those that do. Leafy trailing plants, such as satin pothos, velvet leaf philodendrons, and spider plants, are great plants for propagation by cuttings, but you can experiment with all different types of plants. Succulents are perhaps the easiest to propagate, though not as striking in terms of displaying the process as are leafy foliage plants.

While it sounds counterintuitive, cutting a long trailing plant actually encourages more growth at the top of the plant and aids it in becoming more lush (see Pruning, page 92). Whether you're taking a cutting to propagate, to display simply in a glass jar or vase, or to enhance the growth of the plant, you've got options.

Succulent Propagation

1 Carefully cut a leaf from the stem, making sure to cut as close to the stem as possible. Because many succulent leaves can be removed without scissors, you can also remove one by giving it a gentle twist, being careful not to tear the leaf.

2 Allow the leaf to dry and callous over at the base.

3 Place the calloused leaf atop a shallow layer of damp potting soil in a tray or planter filled with dampened potting soil and spritz with water whenever the soil becomes dry. The tray or planter methods are equally successful, so don't overthink it.

4 Wait for roots and small sprouts to form before repotting (the roots and sprouts will be visible on top of the soil). You may lose a leaf or two when repotting the sprouts due to the fragile nature of succulents, but any fallen leaves can easily be put through the same propagation process to create additional baby plants.

Foliage Propagation

1 Using clean scissors or pruners, cut at a 45-degree angle just below the node (the point where a leaf meets the stem) of a healthy, established stem. Alternatively, you can cut the full stem. This works particularly well with a plant like the Chinese money plant.

2 Remove any lower leaves so that when the cutting is placed in a vase or glass of water, only the nodes are submerged. Any foliage that is submerged will rot.

3 Place the plant cutting in a glass of water. Refresh the water when it becomes cloudy or low (most likely every couple weeks).

4 Allow the cutting to receive moderate to indirect bright light; roots will begin to form from the nodes over the next few weeks to months (some plants root much faster than others). Once the new root system becomes full, you can pot the cutting.

Plant Care

Plants have feelings, too, and for the most part, they love to talk about their feelings, whether they're drooping when they're thirsty or becoming discolored due to light, temperature, watering changes, or pests. Taking care of your plants and giving them the attention they need is therapeutic and rewarding for both you and them. Just as plants acclimate to their new homes, we have to acclimate to them and their care needs. The key to keeping your plants happy is to re-create—as best you can—their native habitat. While that is nearly impossible to do perfectly, it presents a fun challenge and allows you to establish a relationship with your plant.

Light and Temperature

Plants require light to live and thrive. The first step in determining the light in your space is to know which direction your windows face. Bright and direct light is cast by south-facing windows, and that light is accompanied by a lot of heat. Moderate and bright indirect light comes with north- and west-facing windows and tends to be warm but not as hot as direct light. Lower light conditions are provided by east-facing windows, which are also conducive to cooler temperatures. There are plants for every one of these light conditions, so you should have no trouble finding a plant that best suits your space.

The general rule of thumb for temperature is that if you're comfortable, your plants will be comfortable. Indoor plants prefer consistency, and drastic changes in temperature can cause your plants stress. During colder months, try to keep them away from radiators, heating vents, and drafty windows. During warmer months, keep them away from air conditioners and hot windows especially.

Watering

Watering needs depend on the type of plant, light, season, and temperature. When it comes to a schedule, the temperatures both indoors and out will inform your watering throughout the year. On average, most houseplants require watering once every 7 to 10 days. That said, depending on the humidity and temperature in the space, the watering schedule may need to be adjusted. You can check a plant's moisture level by feeling the top inch or two of soil. In most cases, if the soil is moist to the touch, the plant will not need more water. If the soil is completely dry, then your plant is likely thirsty and ready for a watering. Don't hesitate to get in there and really feel the soil because this is the best way to get to know your plant's watering needs. Alternatively, you can stick a wooden chopstick into the soil to gauge the moisture level. If it comes out clean, then it's time to water. If it comes out wet with soil residue, then there's no need to water just yet.

Generally, during hot months and in bright light, plants need more water, whereas during cooler months and in lower light, they require less. It's important to note that in winter, plants may dry out much faster because of their proximity to heating sources. Likewise, plants may dry out fast in summer if the temperatures in your home are warmer due to outside temperatures. With that in mind, even houseplants have periods of dormancy in the colder months, so as long as your home isn't extremely hot, you'll want to provide your plants with less frequent watering. These seasonal changes can throw off a plant's watering schedule, but a quick soil check in between your regularly scheduled watering will keep you in tune with your plant's needs. The most common culprit for plant death is overwatering—so when in doubt, skip a watering or provide a very light watering.

Regular misting or spritzing may also be necessary for plants that typically thrive in humid climates, such as palms or ferns. If your plant is in the bathroom, then you may be off the hook for additional misting. If it's located elsewhere in your home or office, mist or use a humidifier once or twice a week to provide your plant with the humidity and foliar moisture it requires.

General rules of (green) thumb:

- Light and drainage are the most important things to consider.

- Reduce frequency of watering in colder months, but be mindful of plants near heating sources. Soil will dry out at different rates given the temperature in your space.

- Most houseplants don't like wet feet, so water evenly and gradually. If water comes out of the bottom of the drainage hole and fills the saucer, make sure the plant is not sitting in water for too long, which could cause root rot. The plant will stop taking up water when its thirst has been quenched, typically after 15 minutes or so. Discard excess water from saucer.

- If your planter does not have a drainage hole, water lightly and in a couple half-hour increments. This allows the plant to gradually take up the water without the water rushing to and sitting at the base of the planter.

- Use water at room temperature.

- Try to keep a regular watering schedule, ideally in the morning in an effort to allow the soil to dry throughout the day.

Fertilizing

Think of fertilizer as a multivitamin for your plants. Over time, the plants will take up many of the nutrients from the soil. Since they aren't gathering nutrients indoors as they would outdoors, feeding them is super helpful. While it's not always necessary to fertilize your plants, fertilizing will help maintain their longevity and give your plants a little energy boost. The best time to fertilize is in the spring, when your plants are waking up after the long winter; from there you can fertilize weekly or even monthly up until the fall; it's up to you and your plant's needs. Fertilizer should be applied sparingly and never on newly potted plants, since the potting alone can be a shock to their system. It's good to fertilize particularly if you feel that your plant has plateaued in terms of new growth, flowering, or fruiting, or if it appears that there might be a nutrient deficiency (yellowing or browning leaves).

When in doubt, skip or go light on the fertilizer. As with watering, it's always best to underfertilize rather than overfertilize. Alternatively, dressing your plant with a fresh layer of soil with slow-release fertilizer on top may be enough to reinvigorate your plant. For other soil amendment options that are not technically fertilizers, worm castings, eggshells, or a fish emulsion provide nutrients to your plants in a gentle but useful way.

Pruning

Pruning your houseplants is not only a good practice for the growth of your plant but is useful for aesthetic purposes as well. While not all plants benefit from pruning, such as palms, it encourages more plant growth and allows the plant to become fuller. Pruning can also be done to remove dried or discolored foliage or if pests have commandeered areas of your plant. When pruning, it's best to use clean, sharp sheers or pruners and remove foliage from just before a node or as close to the main stem as possible. If just a small portion of the foliage is discolored, only remove the discolored bit, being careful not to cut into the healthy, green foliage.

Pests

The ecosystem needs pests, but your houseplants don't. They're inevitable and come hand in hand with being a plant parent. Like humans, plants have their ailments, and while pests on houseplants are manageable, there's no denying that they can be very persistent and stubborn and pose quite the challenge. With the right tools, some elbow grease, positive thinking, and determination, you and your plants can overcome these pesky little buggers.

Common houseplant pests:

- **Spider Mites:** These tiny red mites typically leave a light webbing on the undersides of leaves and may cause them to yellow. They are difficult to see with the naked eye, but you can test for them by placing a white piece of paper under a leaf and gently flicking the top of the leaf. Take a close look at the paper to see if you notice any movement of small brownish-red specks on the paper. If you do, you may have spider mites. Wipe all the leaves with insecticidal soap or neem oil once every 1 to 2 weeks until the plant stabilizes and ceases turning yellow.

- **Thrips:** Signs of a thrip infestation are yellow, blotchy spots on leaves and leaf drop. Thrips are so tiny that they're nearly impossible to see, but if you look closely and in the right light, you'll see their black or yellow slender bodies on the foliage. If you're uncertain of whether you have a thrip issue, use the same method as for the spider mites (above) and tap the leaf over a white piece of paper to see if you spot any tiny moving specks. Beneficial nematodes are at the top of my list for ridding plants of thrips. They can be found at most plant nurseries, and they're introduced into the soil so that they can attack the pests without damaging the plant itself.

- **Mealy Bugs:** These resemble white cotton at the leaf and stem junction. Gently remove them using a cotton swab soaked with rubbing alcohol. Wiping the affected areas with neem oil or an insecticidal soap will help repel future infestations.

- **Fungus Gnats:** These tiny larvae infest moist potting mix, while mature gnats cause quite a nuisance by flying around your home. Serious infestations can stunt the growth of plants and feed on tender plant roots, though they are not too harmful. Reduce the moisture in the soil by letting your plants dry out in between watering. BTi (*Bacillus thuringiensis* subsp. *israelensis*) or beneficial nematodes added to the soil also help to kill the larvae, and a sticky trap near the plant will aid in killing the adults that are flying around.

- **Scale:** These pests can be hard to see on woody plants, but they will secrete a sticky honeydew, alerting you to their presence. Otherwise, look for yellowing leaves or premature leaf dropping as a warning sign. The adults are immobile pests that attach themselves to leaves or stems. They have protective, hard, brown disk-shaped exteriors, and they can be removed using a knife or your fingernail to gently scrape them off. You can also treat them by wiping all the leaves and stems with insecticidal soap or neem oil once every 1 to 2 weeks until you see the occurrence of scale subside and your plant's health shows no further signs of stress.

General pest management rules:

- If you've adjusted the watering due to clear signs that your plant is stressed, try giving your plants a shower. Most plant pests are tiny and difficult to see with the naked eye, so giving the foliage (not the soil) a good rinse or wipe down can help eradicate or at least minimize harmful pests.

- Quarantine any plants with pests so the pests don't migrate and infest other neighboring plants.

- Spray afflicted plants with DIY insecticidal soap every 1 to 2 weeks, which you can make by combining 1 quart of water with 1 tablespoon of castile soap (such as Dr. Bronner's). For a tougher solution, add 1 tablespoon of cooking oil, such as vegetable, canola, or safflower oil, to the mix and shake the bottle before spraying. Neem oil is also a stellar solution to managing pests and is easily applied by spraying the plant's foliage and stems.

- Badly infested plants will most likely need to be thrown out, though it's generally worth a few treatments to try to save your plant before giving up. Don't hesitate to throw in the towel for any plants that you feel are too far gone. Just be sure to carefully dispose of the plant and thoroughly wash the planter it was in before potting a new plant in it.

Plant care troubleshooting:

Plants will have highs and lows with their health, but it's all part of the process. Plants will let you know when they're feeling unwell, and as long as you're paying attention, there are some ways to navigate their stress and nurse them back to health. Some common signs of stress follow.

- Shriveled, limp, or drooping leaves are often an indication that your plants are thirsty or have pests.

- Yellowing leaves can be a sign of overwatering, mineral deficiency, an issue with temperature, or pests.

- Browning, crisp leaves can be a sign of underwatering, lack of humidity, or sunburn.

- Black, mushy leaves or stems can be an indication of root rot.

- Spotted leaves can be a sign of the plant reacting to overwhelming amounts of minerals, salt, or chlorine in your tap water. If possible, try switching to distilled water or allowing your tap water to sit in the watering can for 24 hours before watering.

- If your plant is leaning significantly in one direction, try rotating it. A leaning plant is typically an indication that it is reaching toward the light. Rotating it will help even out the growth for a more symmetrical shape.

About the Author

Lisa Muñoz is a Brooklyn-based interior plant designer and owner of Leaf and June. The name Leaf and June combines Lisa's nickname, Leaf, and her influential maternal grandmother's first name, June. She started gardening as a child alongside her grandparents in San Antonio, Texas. Lisa earned her certificate in horticulture at the Brooklyn Botanic Garden in 2013 and continues to learn something new about plants every single day. Her work includes indoor plant design and container gardening for residential and commercial spaces. Leaf and June has been featured in the *New York Times*, *Architectural Digest*, *Vogue*, *New York Magazine*, and *Design Sponge*.

Besides having a green thumb, Lisa has a passion for visual design, and her business savvy is grounded in fourteen years of experience as an animation, motion design, and visual effects producer.

Unsurprisingly, she has been known to name her plants . . . usually after dear relatives and music artists.

Acknowledgments

Thank you to the team at Ten Speed, without whom this book would not exist. You all believed in me, rallied behind my ideas, and supported me every single step of the way. To Kaitlin Ketchum, Lisa Regul, Want Chyi, and Emma Campion, thank you for being so detailed, asking all the right questions, getting excited about plants (it's infectious!), and holding my hand throughout a completely new process for me. I can't thank you enough for making this all happen so seamlessly.

Thanks also to photographer Erin Kunkel for sharing your home and capturing plants so beautifully. Thank you to Natasha Kolenko for helping to style this book and being an extra set of eyes and hands throughout the shoot. Thank you to Settlewell, Lightly, and Hudson and Oak for your support and gorgeous planters. Big thanks also to Cactus Jungle, Delano Nursery, Flora Grubb, Plants and Friends, and Sloat Garden Center for the beautiful plants.

Thank you to my family; my partner in life, pasta, and plant parenting, David Azzoni; and Marty, our scruffy dog, who snuggled up next to me throughout the writing process. To my madre; dad; sister, Lori (aka Manzanita Roja); stepdad, Gerald; and stepmom, Betty: you have my heartstrings. Thanks also to my dear friends who encouraged me to write about plants, and many thanks to those who helped guide, proofread, and cheer me on along the way—Felix Cabrera, Valentina Savarese, Elena Azzoni, Christine Hernandez, and Doan Ly. Thanks to my grandparents, June and Bill and Rafaela and Frank, for always being so passionate about your gardens throughout my childhood. You left a lasting impression on how wonderful and inspiring plant life is, and I'm thankful it stuck with me all these years. Thank you to Radiolab and Oliver Sacks for keeping my brain stimulated and curious. Thank you to my plant and record collections for keeping me motivated and moving forward. And last but certainly not least, thank you to my plants. We've been through it all together, haven't we? And we just keep on keeping on.

Plant Photography Index

Index

Published in the United States by Ten Speed Press, an imprint of Random
House, a division of Penguin Random House LLC, New York.
www.tenspeed.com

Ten Speed Press and the Ten Speed Press colophon are registered
trademarks of Penguin Random House LLC.

Library of Congress Cataloging-in-Publication Data
Names: Muñoz, Lisa, author.
Title: House planted : choosing, growing, and styling the perfect plants for
    your space / Lisa Muñoz.
Description: First edition. | New York: Ten Speed Press, [2021] | Includes index.
Identifiers: LCCN 2020042824 (print) | LCCN 2020042825 (ebook) | ISBN
    9780399580840 (hardcover) | ISBN 9780399580857 (ebook)
Subjects: LCSH: House plants in interior decoration. | House plants.
Classification: LCC SB419.25 .M866 2021 (print) | LCC SB419.25 (ebook) |
    DDC 635.9/65—dc23
LC record available at https://lccn.loc.gov/2020042824
    LC ebook record available at https://lccn.loc.gov/2020042825

Hardcover ISBN: 978-0-399-58084-0
eBook ISBN: 978-0-399-58085-7

Printed in China

Photo on page 98: David Azzoni
Acquiring editor: Kaitlin Ketchum | Project editor: Lisa Regul
Editorial assistant: Want Chyi
Designer and art director: Emma Campion | Production designers: Mari Gill
and Mara Gendell
Production manager: Dan Myers
Prepress color: Jane Chinn
Prop stylist: Natasha Kolenko
Photo assistant: Kala Minko
Copyeditor: Andrea Chesman | Proofreader: Kathy Brock
Indexer: Ken DellaPenta
Publicist: Jana Branson | Marketer: Andrea Portanova

10 9 8 7 6 5 4 3 2 1

First Edition